Sis, Be Nicer to Yourself

How Self-Sabotage and Codependency Block You from Manifesting Love, Happiness and Money

RAINIE HOWARD

Also by Rainie Howard:

ADDICTED TO PAIN

YOU ARE ENOUGH

DECIDING TO LOVE

WHEN GOD SENT MY HUSBAND

UNDENIABLE BREAKTHROUGH

MIRACLES IN YOUR MOUTH

Howard Global Enterprises Publishing Agency

For information about special discounts for bulk purchases or bringing the author to your live event, please contact Rainie Howard Enterprises Sales
at 314-827-5216 or Contact@RainieHoward.com
Manufactured in the United State of America

ISBN:

DEDICATION

THIS BOOK IS DEDICATED TO EVERYONE
ASKING AND SEEKING A LIFE MORE
ABUNDANTLY.

TABLE OF CONTENTS

———— ❧��� ————

INTRODUCTION

You have been pushing yourself for so long. Working hard to be the best, look your best and act to impress. You are a fighter. You've been fighting and striving for so long and now you are tired. Yet you hide your fatigue behind to-do lists, college degrees, job promotions and lip gloss smiles. You seek the love of a significant other to rescue you. You hide behind the loneliness of your daily grind.

The truth is you are tired. You are tired of the heartbreak, broken promises, dried-up dreams and disappointing defeats.

You've been struggling to get things up and off the ground and now you ask, "When will I soar?"

You've been taught by society to become likable, struggle for your success, sacrifice your happiness to make sure others are happy, work harder and compete with everyone else while striving each day to be the best at what you do— even though you hate your job.

Sis, trust me . . . I can relate. I also fell into that trap of the struggle, sacrifice, and pain mentality. I struggled as a people pleaser seeking the validation and approval of others; striving for more recognition and accolades to prove my worth. That mindset led to a difficult, hard, and depressing life. I would push myself beyond my capacity and then get upset with myself because I became tired, fatigued, stressed and anxious.

What was wrong with me? Why did life seem like such a struggle and why did it seem different for others? All around me people were thriving. Why couldn't I be happy like them? Why couldn't I lose the weight I struggled to get off for years? Why couldn't I enjoy a loving happy relationship, and thrive in financial abundance? Why did it seem so easy for other people to prosper so effortlessly while I depleted myself struggling just to survive?

Was I not smart enough, pretty enough, or spiritual enough? I wondered if I should pray more, study more or give more. I thought maybe if I tried harder things would get better.

For years, the harder I tried the further I felt away from my dream life. The dream I envisioned for myself was beautiful. I wanted more, I desired passion, love excitement and prosperity. I wanted to enjoy myself, I wanted to love the way I look and radiate confidence. I wanted more excitement and adventure in my life and the more I thought about what I wanted the more miserable I felt. You may be like me constantly telling yourself, "One day things will get better." Every day you wake up looking for things to improve and no matter how many improvements you make you always feel decades behind what you really desire.

Let's expose those questions that you have in your mind like, "Why did he leave me, why did my marriage fail, why can't I maintain a loving relationship or why am I broke and barely have enough money to pay all my bills? Why is it so difficult to lose weight or why do people take advantage of me and use me or why when good things happen for me they never last?"

Whether you are aware of it or not, you are living in a spiritual environment. We are often programmed to observe and only be aware of the physical.

We trust more in our physical senses to see, hear, smell, taste, and touch but we often ignore our spiritual senses. We have spiritual senses such as intuition, imagination, will, reason, perception, and memory. Just as our physical senses help us to properly navigate through this physical world our spiritual senses assist us in navigating through the spiritual (unseen) atmosphere of this world. Because the big truth is, although we can't physically see the spiritual realm, we all feel it.

We feel it in the atmosphere as we go throughout our day. We can feel the tension, uneasiness, uncertainty, stress, fear and even panic. We feel it watching the news, we feel it in politics, we feel it talking to our friends and family. It's felt in education, the economy, and at work. We can't physically see the spiritual energy we feel but we can all feel it. The fact that we cannot tangibly grab a hold of it is the reason many people ignore it, or they distract their minds away from the spiritual reality that is present all around. Most people don't realize it's unavoidable. It's never-ending—it always is and always will be. They hide from it using various substances to escape, numbing their feelings with overeating, drugs, alcohol, and sex. Some people hide from it by becoming busy, high achieving, and overconsuming themselves with work and the pursuit of big accomplishments. They run from it telling themselves if only I fall in love, make millions of dollars, or lose the weight it will all get better. If only I buy the house, the brand-new luxury car, and build the business it will all be better. If only I take the vacation and travel the world it will all feel better. Some people use religion to escape the feeling. They become addicted to their rituals and obsessive over their religious practice. Some people rely on others. They become addicted to people-pleasing and codependent relationships. They rely more on the approval of others and external validation.

Some people become obsessed with "manifesting" things, and they indeed start physically manifesting things they desire yet they are left with feelings of irritation and uneasy distress which ultimately leads to sabotaging the very thing they manifested. Although they have the physical manifestation they wanted, they are still dealing with the unwanted feelings that ultimately end up sabotaging the physical manifestation or even creating other unwanted physical manifestations in addition to the desired ones. You may be thinking: but isn't this book about manifesting and isn't it good for me to manifest my desires? Yes, this book will teach on manifesting, however, there is a proper way to the manifesting process and your motives and spiritual alignment are very important. Many manifesting methods and books teach you to focus on the external things you are seeking to manifest and although that is part of the process; that's not the most important component. You must also learn to not only manifest what you want physically but understand and be aware of what you're manifesting spiritually. Everything seen came from the unseen which is spiritual.

It is when you stop and ask yourself, after doing all that I can to improve my life; am I still struggling with fear, worry, anxiety, uncertainty, unworthiness, and unfulfillment? If the answer is yes, you have been depending on those things to bring you freedom and they have done nothing but distracted you from the abundant life you truly desire.

True abundance is a state of mind, it is intentional purpose with little to no hard work. It's effortless, it comes with ease. It's a playful, fun and childlike faith that's full of joy and grace. It is only this state of mind that guides and directs one to riches, love, and well-being. You have the power and ability to flow into this abundant life if you are willing to stop resisting it. If you are willing to let go of the energy of control that is fighting the fear, worry and stress and begin to allow the flow of God (divine source of infinite intelligence) to guide you—then abundant life will flow to you. When you let go and align your thoughts with the divine, your thoughts will be like God's thoughts. You will be sailing through the eternal waters of life dwelling in the presence of God. Abiding in the oneness of all truth and wisdom. As you are one with the Almighty you become one with abundance and this is how you attract abundance. This abundance comes when you are conscious (awake and aware) of it.

Wealth comes to those who become wealth conscious. Love comes to those who are love conscious. Your thoughts combined with your strong desire has a tendency to transform itself into the physical equivalent. You have the power to transform your definite purpose of desire for love, money and good health into the physical reality of its manifestation. Thoughts become physical reality. Your mental vision that happens first in your mind will one day become real in the physical world if you combine it with emotion and persistence.

"Our life is what our thoughts make it." – James Allen

"Thoughts become things. If you see it in your mind, you will hold it in your hand." – Bob Proctor

When it comes to manifesting you can "control" your thoughts through various techniques. You can "trick" your mind into believing anything through the repetition of affirmations and auto-suggestion and one day you can look up and see physically you are living the life of your dreams. However, if while you're reprogramming your mind with everything you want; you are also avoiding, ignoring and hiding from the spiritual (unseen) negative emotions you refuse to face—they will also participate in the creation and manifestation process. You must address them and do the necessary work to uproot the negative unwanted emotions, heal and replace them with what you truly desire.

Taking control of your mind is the foundation of attracting abundance, love and happiness. We don't have control over the economy, we don't have control over other people and their decisions but there's one thing we do have control over—our mind. Instead of focusing on controlling everything outside of you, put your focus on controlling your mind only. When you gain control of your mind, you gain control of your life.

Control your mind, control your destiny.

The teachings in this book will unveil the true nature of your super powerful spirit. It is a state of calm, strength and universal authority that is capable of overcoming all things. You will begin to understand that the victimization mindset programmed by society and social norms is not who you are.

The mindset of lack, struggle, poverty and scarcity are all illusions we were taught to believe in. We attached ourselves to them and took them on as our true identity. They are not who we are. We are abundant, prosperous and courageous.

As you read this book combine the knowledge and information with self-development to work on reprogramming your self-image to a higher level than what you are seeking to attract. See yourself as more than worthy of all of it. Otherwise, unworthiness and low self-image will sabotage your success. Understand your value and wholeness with or without the physical manifestation.

In other words, the wealth you desire, the relationship you dream of and the fit healthy body you want; does not add value to who you are. You must see you, yourself alone much more valuable than all of it. Your self-image should be outrageously beyond anything you desire externally. What you want to manifest does not make you or break you.

You are unbreakable.

CHAPTER 1

─────── ✥✣✥ ───────

STOP PLAYING SMALL

For some reason, it felt normal to struggle. It seemed to be common to be going through hardship and pain. It was almost like being happy, successful, in love, wealthy and physically fit was for arrogant people.

In my mind, good people went through pain. Good people gave their last and good people didn't strive for more because good people should always be happy settling in their current situation. It was the mentality of "you should just be happy with where you are because it can always be worse." This mindset came from my childhood programming that I should accept life as it is, be happy with what I had and eat my food even if I didn't like it because there are starving babies in Africa. This led to me feeling guilty anytime I wanted something beyond the norm. I felt guilty for not enjoying what I had. As a child, I had big dreams. I envisioned myself as a successful model and fashion designer. I daydreamed about traveling the world and living a fun joyful life. However, as I got older my childhood dreams felt more like a fantasy. The world taught me to be "realistic" and stop dreaming. People respect you more when you sacrifice your dreams, get a college degree and work a decent paying job, and for years, I believed the messages of society. It felt like I was at odds with myself. There was a part of me that said, "Follow your heart, be led by your passion" and another part of me saying, "Don't be crazy, focus on paying bills and working that job." For years, my mental programming of denying myself won. I was in a cycle of playing it small. I was guided by anxiety, fear, guilt and responsibility.

Your own worst enemy

I became my own worst enemy. Instead of prioritizing the health of my mind, body and spirit, I looked out for everybody else. I was focused on making sure my husband and kids, friends and relatives were happy. I became a professional people pleaser. I often felt that because people knew I was reliable, nice and humble, they could get what they wanted from me even if it didn't serve me in any way. It wasn't until years later when I started prioritizing my self-care and putting myself first that I experienced a major difference in the way people treated me. People showed me so much love, honor and appreciation after my self-love growth. I learned that my high level of self-love influenced the quality of my relationships. However, during the years of personal neglect, I attracted users, manipulators, predators, jealous people and toxic, insecure individuals. Some of these people were considered friends, associates, business colleagues and some were family. At that time in my life, I had no idea how much toxic energy I was inviting into my life. I was not aware how playing it small for myself caused me to become my worst enemy. I was my worst enemy not because I deliberately bashed myself but because I deliberately befriended people who were against me, and I didn't even know. I consistently opened the doors of my life to people who despised me and the mind-blowing thing about it, I was addicted to their approval and validation. I hungered for their acceptance not knowing that they were against me. The more I needed their approval the more the lack of it magnified.

I would find myself crying, heartbroken and painfully hurt—often laying on the floor of my room praying to God that He would help me. People often betrayed me, used me and some even lied on me and I would be so mad at myself for being deceived by their fakeness. I often discerned small hints of their deception or what some may call "red flags," but I would always overlook it because their validation was much more important to me.

Low Self-Esteem and Insecurity

My lack of clarity to protect myself from toxic people led to low self-esteem and insecurity. I didn't trust myself to make the best decisions. Life seemed difficult and the more challenging it felt, the harder it got. It became hard to lose weight and be healthy and fit. It was hard to earn extra money and it was a struggle to maintain healthy relationships. I and my husband argued a lot, I often complained that he wasn't romantic enough and one day he told me he was unhappy and considered divorce.

I was miserable, overweight, tired, stressed and broke but I was the most genuine kindhearted person you would ever meet. Why was I so unhappy despite having such a pure and honest loving heart? I wanted to overcome the feelings of turmoil so badly, but it seemed the harder I tried the more I failed. This disappointment led to a dark season of depression and anxiety.

The depression was so severe that I began creating a morning routine just to survive the day. I would do something every morning to nurture my mind, body and spirit. Morning after morning I would start my day speaking positive affirmations, meditating, and writing a gratitude prayer list, which included things I was thankful for that I had and things I was thankful for that I was believing God would provide. That was the practice that nurtured my spirit. Then I would get ready and go to the gym and sometimes to the park to nurture my body through exercise. While exercising I would nurture my mind by listening to motivational messages, audiobooks and podcasts. It became a daily mind, body and spirit ritual and little by little my entire life transformed. I started falling in love with my own company and for the first time in my life, I started enjoying my time all by myself. I looked forward to "me-time"; I became a new person and little by little I started to like myself more.

One day during my morning routine after listening to a motivational message about making the decision in your mind to change, I received a burning desire. For the first time in my adult years, I gave myself permission to be healthy and fit, financially wealthy and successful. I made up my mind that I would be happy, healthy and wealthy. I felt the power of my inner being rise up inside of me and I began to take control of my life and allow myself to experience the life I really desired. That decision was the beginning of turning my life completely around and from then on, I continued to manifest the life I've always dreamed of.

Don't Engage in Negative Self-Talk

My daily intentional decision-making led me to attracting my personal trainer. I started working out 6–7 times a week. I would work out with my trainer two days a week and on the other days I worked out by myself. I started learning the best foods to eat for my body and how to eat clean. I continued my morning routine every day; it was now my lifestyle. My everyday reality began to gradually reflect the dream life I envisioned and desired for so many years. I lost over 30 pounds, my business revenue successfully improved, and my marriage had been restored. Things were going great, and I became hungry for even more. I started setting bigger goals but every time I pushed myself to desire more those past negative thoughts would come up. The thoughts of doubt, fear and defeat. I found myself engaging in negative self-talk. You can't afford to live the life you desire? You lost weight but your belly is still flabby. You are still far away from your goal. How are you going to make that money? You've never made that amount of money. You are still figuring things out. What would people think when you change? They may not like the new you.

Sometimes I was unaware of the negative self-talk, but I would always become aware of how bad it made me feel. Whenever I recognized that I was feeling bad I would identify the negative thought and then work to replace it with a positive thought that reinforced my desire.

Change Your Inner Voice

The battle in my mind led me to learn how to change my inner voice. I began to align with what God says about me and ignore and no longer believe or receive anything that was out of alignment with the abundant life I'm meant to live. So, I allowed myself to dream big.

"The best there is to have is the best for me. The best there is to be is the best for me." – Maya Angelou

So, I went big, and I created big goals I wanted to manifest. My desire was to impact and inspire millions of people through my business, move into my dream home and open a new business facility and warehouse. I wanted to manifest it all in one year. Those goals were so big to me that they scared me. I had no idea how I would manifest them but deep down inside the depths of my soul, I knew it was possible, so I started the manifestation process. I'll share more details of this technique later in another chapter.

I allowed myself to be led by inspired action (in spirit) or in other words spirit led. I began following my intuition, which led me to live by faith and not by sight. I took several leaps of faith that led to manifestations. I manifested my dream car, which is a luxury brand car I had desired for years. In my business, I manifested profitable income to invest in scaling my business which resulted in hiring a business mentor, moving into a temporary small office and hiring an assistant. My husband and I started touring homes that looked like our dream home regardless of the price. My spirit guided me to stop making decisions based on my current income and start surrounding myself with exactly what I desired. My morning routine evolved to reading my goals daily and visualizing and feeling myself living as if it was already done.

I felt so close to my manifestations and one day I had a strong desire to take a vacation. I followed my intuitive guidance and booked a romantic dream vacation for my husband and me. That vacation felt amazing. I remember feeling so free, fun and grateful. Life began to feel amazing. During that trip, there were times I felt like a playful happy kid again. It felt like my big manifestations were closer and closer.

Shortly after my husband and I returned home from our dream trip the entire country closed down. Due to the COVID-19 pandemic, we were advised to quarantine. The government officials mandated that we do not leave the house, not even for work. It felt like my entire world came crashing down. We were told we could only go to the grocery store. So many negative thoughts consumed me. You'll never manifest your dreams now. Your business is probably going to close. You have office space and now you are not supposed to leave home. You should have kept your business at home. Now you have to work from home again. You should go ahead and give up on those goals and stop dreaming. Get your mind back on the reality of things, you are not meant for that dream life, it's unrealistic.

We were planning to move and had been looking for our dream home for months and now everything was locked down. No more touring beautiful homes, we were in quarantine, and no one wants strangers touring their house during a pandemic. I felt stuck. How in the world am I going to manifest the things I desired during a pandemic? At that time no one alive had ever experienced life during a pandemic, it had been over one hundred years since the last one. Manifesting my dreams seemed impossible.

Although the pandemic set me back for a couple of weeks, my morning routine was also my lifestyle habit. I started back nurturing my mind, body and spirit every day. On the outside I was petrified but, on the inside, my inner being was calm and secure.

During my morning meditation and prayer, I heard a small inner voice say, "Trust me, it's coming. You are so close to manifesting everything you desire." In the physical realm, everything looked defeated.

The house we were living in began to fall apart. Leaking walls and a family of raccoons moved into the roof and walls of the house. I wasn't sure how we would operate our business since we were not considered "essential." Yet I maintained my state of calm and faith; I would consistently visualize living in my new house. I would tell my children we are now living in our new house.

They would look at me like I was crazy. Since the gyms were closed, I began taking walks in neighborhoods that had houses like the one I was believing for. On these walks, I would envision myself living in my big, beautiful dream house. I envisioned myself operating a large successful e-commerce company overseeing an amazing staff fulfilling orders and successfully operating effectively. I saw large trucks pulling in supplying our warehouse. I saw myself manage everything with ease.

Never in a million years would I imagine we would be living in a pandemic. I didn't understand it at all, yet a fire in me told me to keep the faith. Something in me said you're going to move in May. One day in April while driving around neighborhoods with my husband sightseeing homes, he received a text from an unknown real estate agent asking if we were still looking for a house. We scheduled a tour to see a home that was not listed yet for sale. When we arrived, we knew it was the dream home my husband and I both envisioned; it had everything we desired. We immediately put in our offer and contract and at the end of May, we moved into our dream home. As for the business, our e-commerce store grew during the pandemic and reached the revenue goal beyond my expectation. We exceeded our annual income goal. We also moved the entire business headquarters from a small 200 square foot office into a 2,500 square foot facility and warehouse. Each and every goal I desired manifested.

I shared this to inspire you to not play it small and allow yourself to dream, envision and evolve, through the journey of self-care and love. As you take care of yourself, life will mirror that and take care of you.

Now, let's talk about how self-sabotage can reverse your manifestation and lead to defeat.

JOURNAL

————— ❧❦❧ —————

Earlier, I shared my experience of attracting toxic people and inviting toxic energy into my life without being aware and I became my own worst enemy. Can you relate to a time in your life when you were your worst enemy?

_____

_____

_____

_____

_____

Do you ever struggle with low self-esteem and insecurity? If so, what are the thoughts that caused it?

_____

_____

_____

_____

_____

Whenever you find yourself engaging in negative self-talk, how will you overcome that toxic thinking?

_____

_____

_____

_____

_____

What do you plan to do in order to change your inner voice to one of love, acceptance and positivity?

_____

_____

_____

_____

_____

"Don't let instant gratification make you forget what has happened in your favor. Enjoy the simple blessings of everyday life."

CHAPTER 2

MANIFEST WITHOUT SABOTAGE

Even after manifesting some good in your life, you can sabotage it all because of your belief pattern. It's the reason why 70% of all lottery winners go broke and a third declare bankruptcy, according to the National Endowment for Financial Education. It's another reason why over 50% of marriages end in divorce. You can fall in love, marry the love of your life and sabotage the entire marriage causing it to end in divorce. Self-sabotage happens when you deliberately destroy the very thing you desire knowingly or subconsciously.

We have all been programmed to think a certain way. As a baby, you were more connected to your true divine nature. However, after years of picking up mindset beliefs from your parents, relatives, friends, teachers and the cultural norms of society, you now have a belief pattern that's influenced in so many ways. Now, when you think of your desire for peace, love, joy, prosperity, abundance and happiness you are in conflict with why you can't maintain the amazing state you desire and why it feels like a struggle.

Why does it feel like a struggle to be in love, why does it feel like a struggle to have financial abundance and why does it feel like a struggle to be happy and enjoy your life in a state of peace and calm?

The reason it's a struggle is because you're not naturally aligned to easily receive those things. For so long you have been conditioned and aligned to struggle, striving and going through pain in order to feel some level of peace or accomplishment.

Think about it, you probably learned stress from your parents. You saw them getting stressed over bills, arguing and yelling when things weren't going their way.

If you truly understood how powerful you are you would never doubt your capability to have any and everything your heart desires. But you don't know, your mind has been conditioned to believe in what you see physically and to know and understand yourself based on what you've done before. It's as if the past has been the predictor of your future. If all you've ever seen was people struggling and barely make it from day to day and if all you've ever done was struggle, strive and stretch yourself only to be in the same position year after year, that becomes your truth and your reality. Many people settle for that reality and unhappiness, as joy and fulfillment seem impossible.

You may have had a very strong desire to manifest love, but you can't stop ignoring and pushing away potential partners. Or maybe you hate being single but also despise going through the dating process? You may have deep fear and anxiety about falling in love and getting brokenhearted. You may be unaware of your sabotaging behaviors when it comes to relationships.

You may have a strong desire to manifest more income or start a business, but you keep procrastinating in applying for your LLC or getting a website. You also may even want to lose weight and get physically fit, but you avoid working out and eating healthier foods. Understand that just because you have a desire for something great, doesn't mean you have the mindset and habits to manifest and maintain it.

There are three habits that will destroy your manifestations: procrastination, perfectionism and negative self-talk.

Procrastination will keep you living a fantasy. As you start the process of manifesting you will begin to receive inspirational ideas and small gut feeling desires to start the momentum. If you are a procrastinator those ideas will come and go. If you don't take immediate steps implementing the inspired ideas, you will stop the flow of manifestation.

Manifesting is about alignment; therefore, procrastination kills the alignment and the necessary growth progress. Procrastinators constantly put things off which causes them to lose focus of their vision. Focusing on your vision is a key component of manifesting your desires. Your consistent everyday focus is the drive you need to build the momentum and maintain the flow of the manifestation of ideas, visions and divine connections. Some people choose to procrastinate because they believe they work better under pressure. Whether you believe this way or not, adding pressure and urgency to the manifestation process will also hinder your alignment. You will start building momentum and alignment with the feelings of stress and pressured anxiety which will ultimately lead you to manifest situations and experiences that magnify more and more pressure.

Perfectionism comes from a deep desire to avoid failure and harsh judgment from others. Perfectionists are often quick to find fault and are often very critical of others and themselves. These people have an unrealistic desire to be perfect. They hold themselves to a really high standard and seeks to control their world. Perfectionism is usually rooted in self-distrust. A major reason why perfectionism will destroy your manifestations is because of your high standards and perfectionist expectations of yourself, and you never feel worthy of allowing and receiving the love and abundance you desire. Perfectionists go throughout life aiming to achieve but never accomplishing their desires. Although they try so hard to be perfect and follow all the steps and rules, they are never really happy. As a perfectionist, you put more energy into getting things right. For example, instead of meditating, journaling and using the visualization techniques to align with your inner being and connect with infinite intelligence, you do those things to punish yourself in a sense to be perfect. You may feel like you have failed too many times, or you're not who you want to be, so you punish and deprive yourself with perfect actions; that's not true alignment. Become ok with the imperfect things that come your way. Don't take life so seriously and stressful. Be nicer to yourself. Enjoy yourself and have fun. The manifestation process feels so good when you allow yourself to be authentically *you*.

Negative self-talk will also steal your manifestations. No matter how many steps you take moving forward to your manifestation, once you start engaging in negative self-talk, you will automatically take ten steps backwards. When people are against you it can be discouraging, however, nothing, and no one can set you back as much as your own negative thoughts about yourself. It's important to understand that negative self-talk is a weapon against your desired manifestation. But it's also important to not beat up on yourself because you have some unwanted emotions or negative thoughts. Celebrate yourself for being aware of it and re-aligning yourself to what serves you better. The purpose of this is to shine a light on what's best for you and open up your awareness to that truth—the more you are loving and caring towards yourself throughout this process, the better you will feel. As you feel better you manifest better.

The ultimate key to overcoming self-sabotage is creating a space of acceptance and love for yourself. The more you allow yourself to receive your own love and acceptance the more you increase your self-image, self-worth and self-trust. That is what's necessary to attracting and manifesting the life you desire. It starts with your relationship with yourself. This process leads you to learning how to tap in and listen from within yourself.

Your Worst Critic

Melissa is a client I was working with for years. When we started coaching sessions, she shared that she had been in two failed marriages. The first marriage ended after five years due to infidelity. Her husband cheated on her, and she was so devastated after the divorce that she quickly got into a rebound relationship with another man who soon after became her second husband. She had children with the second husband and after several years of marriage her second husband was caught cheating on her, and he also had a child with another woman during their marriage.

Melissa stated that the same pain she felt from the first marriage resurfaced but this time it was magnified. She was so upset with herself because she couldn't understand why she didn't see the warning signs until it was too late.

As we worked through the self-care sessions, Melissa discovered how toxic she was towards herself. She had often felt like a failure. She talked about her low self-esteem that followed her throughout her childhood into her adulthood. She talked about how she hated not following through on goals she had in the past and how she often procrastinated when it came to things that could improve her life. She also focused most of her attention on being in a relationship and having a husband. Having a loving romantic relationship was her dominant focus. Her father abandoned her as a young girl, and she often felt like a sad fatherless child. Those thoughts magnified her desire for a husband who would be a loving father for her children. However, during the dating process and even after marriage Melissa was very fearful of losing her husband and when things were going well, she often thought, "this is too good to be true, something bad may happen." That was also a dominant thought that controlled her emotionally and mentally.

One day she asked me, do you think I attracted the infidelity in my marriage with the infidelity beliefs? Did my negative thoughts and fears manifest the pain of both of my divorces? I explained to Melissa the importance of not blaming herself as if she was fully responsible for the infidelity of her relationships. However, our thoughts and beliefs can often sabotage the joy and happiness we desire. Instead of being your worst critic become your greatest cheerleader. Acknowledge the negative belief patterns and become proud of yourself for evolving to that awareness. Now that you are aware of how thoughts become things you can align yourself to positive thoughts and beliefs that serve you better. As you continue the progression of increasing your self-image, self-worth and self-trust you can attract better-feeling thoughts that manifest into better-feeling experiences. Instead of getting upset with yourself because you fear infidelity in your relationship, ask yourself do you believe a loving faithful relationship is possible for you. And you don't, begin the self-worth work of healing the insecurity. As you believe you are worthy you attract relationships and experiences that confirm the worthiness you believe in.

JOURNAL

—————— ❧❦❧❧ ——————

How have you sabotaged yourself in the past and what are the fears you are currently overcoming?

_____

_____

_____

_____

_____

What are the self-sabotaging habits you are overcoming?

_____

_____

_____

_____

_____

"If you really understood how powerful you are you would never doubt your capability to have any and everything your heart desires."

CHAPTER 3

HOW CODEPENDENT RELATIONSHIPS ARE BLOCKING YOUR DESTINY

Codependent relationships are when you excessively rely on another person emotionally and psychologically. It's when you believe you cannot healthily function throughout life without another person. There are two roles of a codependent relationship—the victim and the fixer.

The victim is often the one in need. They justify their toxic behavior and inadequate ways with their past trauma. For instance, one may say, "I'm toxic towards you because I was abused as a child, or I cheated because my ex hurt me and it's hard to trust. I overdrink because my dad abandoned me." The victim is addicted to being recused. They are programmed to rely on another person to fix their situation and they often feel entitled to receiving much more than they contribute. However, the fixer is addicted to solving problems. The fixer is often exhausted and depleted from working so hard to fix everything and everybody. The fixer is addicted to this relationship with the victim because it keeps them busy accomplishing. Fixers love accomplishing things and being the solver of someone else's problems. The fixer becomes too saturated with the problems of the victim that they lose themselves in the mix of fixing things for others. All along the fixer fails to fix their own situation and often don't find any personal character flaws mainly because they are too consumed with the issues of the victim. Both the victim and the fixer are in bondage.

A friend of mine named Lesley was married to Daniel who struggled with alcohol addiction. Daniel would become very verbally abusive to Lesley especially when he was drunk. Lesley dealt with the abuse for years. She often helped Daniel apply for jobs, she would get his clothes ready for work and pack his lunch. She made everything so easy for him. She bought him a new car when his truck broke down. She would always come through for him whenever he needed something. However, she was broken. Daniel said so many demeaning things to her. Lesley started gaining weight and he told her she looked disgusting. He would yell at her when he was drunk, and she found out he cheated on her with one of her friends. Lesley often felt sorry for Daniel because when he was a child his mom died in a fire. He said that's the reason he can't stop drinking. Lesley often said Daniel needed her because he didn't have family. After learning about codependent relationships, Lesley began to realize she was the fixer in her relationship and Daniel was the victim. She was addicted to recusing Daniel from his pain and trauma.

The fixer thinks, "I'll do this to help him now and eventually he will appreciate all that I'm doing, and he will be inspired to change his life and he will get better. One day after changing his life for the better he will remember the role I played and thank me."

The truth is it's a very small chance he will ever make the decision to emotionally and psychologically snap out of the victim mentality and change his life for the better while he has you fully committed to fixing everything. He doesn't want to take full responsibility for solving his own problems because he has you and he's so well programmed to thinking of you (his fixer/problem solver) whenever a problem occurs knowing you will handle it. The painful truth that the "fixer" must understand is that you cannot fix everything and the things you believe you have fixed are temporary tasks that enhance and empower more of you being a fixer and more of him being a victim. You stop the cycle by quitting your role as fixer. You are not destined to be a victim or a fixer. You were created to thrive, and experience life abundantly.

Your life is directly connected to your thoughts. Therefore, regardless of what you're going through in your life make the decision not to be the victim of your thoughts. Decide today to take full ownership of your healing. I want to also encourage you not to fall for the role of the savior. If you want to be a hero, save yourself. Rescue yourself from the toxic pattern of codependent thinking. Detoxify your life from all the drama, lies, abuse and fear.

How Codependency Hinder Manifestations

Codependency keeps you fixated on another person. You are so overly consumed with this other person being the center of your world that you have no room to focus on creating the abundant life you are destined to live.

The drama, toxic behavior and emotional pain of a codependent relationship clouds your foresight and occupies your mind. This blocks your vision, energy and focus while making it feel impossible to even pursue your dream and accomplishing your goals.

However, when it comes to manifesting, the dream life you envision must be fueled by your energy, vision and focused attention.

When it comes to manifesting, it's not just about creating material and physical manifestations (cars, houses, money and relationships, etc.) but most importantly spiritual and mental manifestations (inner peace, healing, calm and well-being etc.). As you focus more on manifesting inner joy and abundance, that loving energy will saturate every area of your life. This will result in a healthier, happy and fulfilled life and as the material manifestations appear your joyful energy will empower you for the enjoyment of both physical and spiritual manifestations.

When it comes to codependent relationships, people often get caught up in seeking physical fulfillment and feeding their flesh while neglecting their spirit. However, as you make your spiritual nourishment a top priority that will be your guide in healthier decisions for yourself. Your healthy mind, body and spirit will guide you to creating healthy boundaries, having high standards and making decisions for the highest good of you and others.

Strengthen Your Self-Worth

Many times, without even realizing it, we connect our identity to external things like other people, jobs, titles and experiences. We take what happened to us and make it our identity. If someone mistreats you, use you or abuse you, you may subconsciously believe you are not valuable because people mistreat you. If you lose your job and struggle to pay your bills you may believe you are broke or in poverty. If one of your close friends suddenly passes away, you may feel like you should have done something to reach out more. We blame ourselves for things out of our control and we create an identity based on our conditions.

Don't you know you are not what happened to you? You are not the titles you've received. You are not the result of a toxic relationship and what happened to you does not define you. You are worth so much more than you realize. Make the commitment to yourself to no longer define yourself by anything that has happened to you. No longer limit yourself to the things your parents told you about yourself—you are so much more than what can be put into words. You are eternal. You are connected to an infinite source, the all-knowing intelligence of almighty God. You are so much more than others can comprehend. As you connect more to your truth and the essence of who you are as an eternal being, you will understand and grow in your self-worth.

Strengthening your self-worth starts with prioritizing your self-care. Self-care is not getting pedicures, massages, new hairstyles and makeup. Self-care is making time to meditate, journal, listen to your desires, envision your dreams, stimulate your mind with personal development books, messages and eating foods that nurture your body, partaking in walking and exercising to circulate your body. Self-care is your lifetime commitment to a healthy mind, body and spirit. As you prioritize "you" above everything else you strengthen your self-worth.

It's the art of knowing the best way to protect yourself, listen to yourself and trust yourself. It's when you evolve to a place where you no longer care what people think about you—because what's important to you is how you see yourself. It's when people come to you bringing up your past and pointing out what they believe as your flaws, but it means nothing to you. The way you know and see yourself is all that matters; that's a very high level of freedom and power. You realize it doesn't matter what they think or say about you, what's most important is what you think and say about yourself.

You strengthen your self-worth as you stop focusing on controlling everything outside of you, and instead put your focus on controlling your mind only. When you gain control of your mind, you gain control of your life. Give up the struggle of trying to control others and their actions and instead focus on filling your mind with positive thoughts, goals and visions that serve you. To start the process of reprogramming your mind, it's important to remember you have to quiet the noise and you do this through meditation. The purpose of meditation isn't to control your thoughts, it's to stop letting your thoughts control you. This is why it's important to create daily self-care habits.

There was a family member who would often trigger me by bringing up negative behavior of my past; I believe because they struggled to understand the new me. In the past, I would have gotten upset and lash out at that person in defense. However, now that I have a daily practice of meditating and I'm really good at not allowing my thoughts to control me, when the relative starts bringing up the past I am able to laugh it off and move forward in conversation without a negative response. When situations like that occur, I'm often very proud of myself and how far I've come in strengthening my self-worth. If you believe you are worth the best, you'll attract the best and you will easily receive the best knowing you are deserving of nothing but the best.

There will be people who will question your receiving of good things. They may wonder if it's right for you to continually enjoy all the good life has to offer.

They may call you lucky, spoiled, privileged and or greedy. That's only because they don't believe they could ever experience so much good. Often, they've lost their own sense of worthiness and life is a difficult struggle from their point of view. Don't spend your time trying to convince them and don't try to justify why it's alright for you to enjoy the best life has to offer. Some things are not meant to be explained. Instead, focus on enjoying your life fully and allowing your happiness, joy and peace of mind to inspire others as you live out your life abundantly.

JOURNAL

———— ❧❧❧ ————

Which role have you played in a relationship, the victim or the fixer?

_____

_____

_____

_____

_____

How will you begin to strengthen your self-worth?

_____

_____

_____

_____

_____

"If you believe you are worth the best, you'll attract the best and you will easily receive the best knowing you are deserving of nothing but the best."

CHAPTER 4

UNLOCK THE ABUNDANCE OF MONEY

"The key to abundance is to meet limited circumstances with unlimited thoughts." – Marianne Williamson

Abundance of wealth starts in your mind. When you let go of mindset limitations, and envision what you desire, see it, feel it and believe it, you will receive it. Your mindset limitations often started during childhood. You were influenced by the people around you. Maybe they struggled with a shortage of money. Maybe your parents or grandparents talked about how hard it was to earn money. You may have grown up watching the people around you struggle to pay bills. These experiences created beliefs that you stored in your subconscious mind, and they often lead to beliefs in scarcity and lack. These beliefs create thoughts in your mind that create other like-minded thoughts that ultimately form into belief patterns. In addition, these belief patterns attract situations, relationships and circumstances that reinforce scarcity and lack. Now, when someone comes to you and says, "There's no such thing as scarcity and you can attract all the money you desire if you work on your mind," you look at them, laugh in disbelief and then try to prove them wrong by showing off your paycheck and bills. Doing this continues the attraction of more and more lack and financial struggle. What if there was a huge chance you could create more financial abundance and enjoy an amazing happy healthy wealthy life? What if you could enjoy receiving money easily and effortlessly? What if you could enjoy money coming abundantly to you even when you are asleep?

If it's possible for others it's possible for you and if you are thinking of the possibility of abundance in your life, it's already a sign that it's for you. The only thing that is holding you back is your own mental limitations.

A No Limit Mindset Attracts Unlimited Money

Let's start by understanding the impact relationships have on you. The jobs, careers, home choices and income of the people around you have a major impact on your mind—and even more so when you were a child. Those things created exposure and oftentimes they set limits and boundaries on what you believed was possible. Even if you allowed yourself to go beyond those mental limitations in some way the fear, self-sabotage and lack of familiarity would cause you to struggle in maintaining that higher level of success.

Attracting wealth is a six-step process like planting a seed that will one day become a plant.

Step 1: Plant the seed in good soil. When it comes to wealth, you want to plant good thoughts in the soil of your mind. Your mind is where the wealthy thoughts are nurtured.

Step 2: Water the seed frequently and keep the soil evenly moist throughout the process. Create a daily habit of sending positive energy to your wealth thoughts. Meditate and envision them as reality in your life. Review your wealth goals and stay focused on living an abundant wealthy life.

Step 3: Understand that the seed is expanding underground and beginning the root system. Your daily habits of directing positive energy to your wealthy thoughts are expanding. You can't see the physical evidence of it yet, but those wealthy thoughts are growing roots. It's all happening in an unseen realm just as the underground growth of the seed.

Step 4: Watch the part of the stem of an embryo plant extending and pushing through the soil to emerge in the air. Your wealth thoughts are now beginning to manifest small physical evidence. You may receive intuitive thoughts that lead to an opportunity that pays your rent or someone gives you a gift card or offers to pay for your meal. Usually, these small manifestations feel nice, but you are still focused on that seed becoming a plant or in other words your wealthy thoughts manifesting as financial abundance. Stay aligned to the good feeling of abundance. That wealth seed still needs lots of watering and nurture.

Step 5: Tiny leaves are beginning to emerge out of the stem. You are now seeing more and more evidence that your seed is growing. You are not only seeing more and more small physical evidence, but you are also feeling a massive amount of emotional evidence. Your faith in these wealth thoughts is stronger than ever before. You have more certainty, and you are starting to feel like the manifestation is done.

Step 6: You are now observing the stem getting taller and taller and the leaves growing larger and larger. As the leaves completely pop out of the covering and the cotyledons separate and fall from the seeding, the development of the plant is complete. You will now observe your wealthy thoughts become things. Your manifestations will become bigger and bigger. The physical manifestations of wealth are completely revealed in abundance.

The process of nature is also the process of manifestation. However, the main reason many people never witness the physical manifestation of their desires is because they don't commit to the development process of maintaining their alignment to the thoughts and beliefs of what they desire. Many people give up because they don't see the physical evidence soon enough or when the small physical evidence starts manifesting, they are ungrateful because it's not as big as they desire it to be.

However, getting upset and mad because it's not happening fast enough is the same as getting upset that the planted seed isn't becoming a plant fast enough and pulling the seed out of the ground in frustration. This is the reason so many people kill their dreams and abort their vision.

Thoughts become words, words become action and action becomes habits and habits form your destiny. It all starts with your mind.

Release Money Blocks

Here is a list of money blocks (thoughts, beliefs and ideas that will sabotage wealth and financial abundance).

- ***The belief that you don't deserve an abundance of money.*** Maybe you grew up believing that wealth was for other people, and you didn't fit the description of someone who could have financial abundance. We often subconsciously pick up beliefs without knowing it and maybe you connected your identity to one who is not financially wealthy. This mindset will block you from receiving wealth.

- ***You fear success.*** Are you afraid that if you become successful it won't last? Do you believe if you attracted a large sum of money, you wouldn't be responsible, and you would struggle to successfully manage it? The fear of success is one of the biggest money blocks that could hold individuals back. Years ago, I personally struggled with the fear of success and after attracting a large amount of money my fear led me to sabotaging my success. It's like I was subconsciously saying I'm not ready yet. After going through that experience, I began doing the things that made me feel more comfortable and ready. I met with a financial advisor, I learned about investing in stocks and real estate and I conditioned myself to be comfortable saving larger sums of money. I needed to prove to myself that I can be my own financial expert and make wise decisions about money. These things helped me to release all fear and build a better relationship with money and success, allowing myself to feel natural with the secure feelings of wealth.

- ***Excessively giving while refusing to receive.*** Manifesting is a process of both giving and receiving. It's a continual circulation of abundance. It's the knowing that as you give, more is coming, and as you receive there are more opportunities to give. It's an ongoing cycle of freedom, the freedom to give and the freedom to receive. However, some people struggle with receiving. This mindset is subconsciously asking for help and support but refusing the opportunities when they arrive. Your value is not tied up in only what you do for others but it's a good thing to allow yourself to receive wonderful things for yourself as well.

There are other money blocks you may not be aware of like having low expectations, lacking clear intentions and

RAINIE HOWARD

ignoring your intuition to take inspired action. It's important to identify what money blocks are holding you back from abundance and begin positioning yourself to receive and allow the flow of wealth. For years I wasn't aware of some of my past money blocks. I began to discover them after paying attention to my thoughts and actions around money. I noticed how in the past whenever I received a large sum of money all at once, I felt the urgency and anxiety to hurry and figure out what to do with it. I felt like if I didn't have a plan for the money then I didn't have a right to have it. Therefore, I expected to be quick in my financial decision-making. That mindset led me to overspending and constantly putting myself in a crunch. I was taking action without alignment. Then one day the revelation came to me, and I realized I didn't have to have a quick plan or spend money quickly. I began to allow myself to savor the feeling of having more than enough money in my bank account and to enjoy not assigning the money to a plan. Instead, I would allow divine guidance and intuition to direct any plans whenever they came. It felt good to maintain financial peace, ease and flow. My energy about money began to align with abundance and well-being. I realized then I had unlocked the abundance of money in my life. This allowed me to understand that my relationship with my own emotional peace, calm and ease

58

impacted my relationship with the ease of my receiving of financial abundance. As I maintain this state of clarity and ease, I'm guided to thoughts, ideas and connections that align with my state in every area of my life including finances.

Don't Cheat Yourself Treat Yourself

Ask yourself, are you comfortable with an abundance of money? If you received a large amount of money today, would you feel inadequate to properly manage it wisely, or would you feel more ready and prepared to be divinely led to make the right decisions?

As you evolve in your self-worth, self-image and self-confidence, your management of financial wealth will evolve. It starts with prioritizing what's best for you. Fall in love with the best version of yourself. Do the things that align with your natural state of peace and calm. Life doesn't need to be a struggle.

Money comes just like ideas come. When an idea comes, it doesn't mean you need to immediately act on that idea. Sometimes you need to sit with the idea for a while and allow more clarity and details to form before you take action. This is true also when an unexpected amount of money manifests in your life. Sit with it for a while, allow it to be in your bank account or your wallet for a bit. Then allow more clarity and guidance to be revealed before you take action; as you do this, you give yourself some time and space to expand in the evolvement of managing the abundance of money. Instead of quickly finding ways to spend it and never allowing yourself to evolve to the level of financial wealth, your patience and alignment of the opportunity prepare you to properly handle it.

Start to make room for the financial abundance you desire because it's on its way. Make room by expanding your mind learning money growth and management techniques. Make room by healing the emotional money blocks and make room by creating an environment that is supportive of a wealthy lifestyle. Organize your living space with images, sounds and fragrances of opulence. Organize your finances with the proper budget and revenue-generating strategy and learn to trust the process. Relax more and trust your intuition. In order to attract wealth, you must align yourself to receive it.

 Money doesn't come just to be spent. Money comes as a result of an abundance mindset that can expand beyond limited circumstances. Always remember manifesting money and material things are great but the ultimate manifestation is having control over the way you feel.

JOURNAL

————— ❧❧❧❧ —————

What are the thoughts and beliefs you have about money that are blocking you from receiving it abundantly?

_____

_____

_____

_____

_____

Are you comfortable with an abundance of money? If you received a large amount of money today, what would you do?

_____

_____

_____

_____

_____

"As you evolve in your self-worth, self-image and self-confidence, your management of financial wealth will evolve."

CHAPTER 5

THE LAW OF ALLOWING

Sometimes growth may feel like you're losing when you are actually aligning and expanding. Growth may lead to ending and removing some people and things. Growth isn't always packaged in rewards. Growth may cause you to end friendships, say no to certain opportunities and eliminate some habits. Just because some things are subtracting from your life doesn't mean you're not growing.

There were times when I was going through a growth season, and it seemed as if everything familiar and comfortable was ending. I didn't understand that the old was making room for the new. However, my old mindset of working hard, struggling and people-pleasing led me to pushing myself to the brink of a burnout. I was hard on myself to the point of having a nervous breakdown. I was sabotaging my success by rushing things, forcing results and chasing instant gratification. I was putting everyone else above my own mental health. I learned very quickly that it was time to create new healthy habits and self-care. I understood the importance of doing things differently in order to expect different results. My vision of my future became my reality instead of the past and the unwanted conditions that had presently manifested.

You must understand that what is, is the enemy of what is to come. It's when you make your vision, your inner voice and your desires a priority—that's when your life begins to shift. Make the decision to choose you. The relationship you have with yourself is what's most important. As you do this you will not need to be validated by others but instead allowing the love for yourself to be enough. You don't have to always be the one giving, fixing, trying and appeasing. You deserve nothing but the best. You are worthy of good. You don't have to work for it, just receive it. You are a new you, now thrive. Stop being the one who's always picking up the pieces and holding everything together. You don't have to be the glue.

Ask and it is given

The moment you ask for what you desire, it's already done. It is immediately complete in the unseen spiritual realm and the reason many people never experience the physical manifestation of their desire is because they do not know how to receive it. Instead of allowing it to manifest and receiving it, doubt and disbelief destroy it before its physical manifestation. We are programmed to give but many of us struggle to receive. Receiving requires alignment and allowing.

Allow things to unfold and be revealed. You alone are enough. Allow you to happen. Let go and be. Feel the feeling of letting go. Release yourself from the duty of making things right and working things out. That mindset influences you and leads you to cling to and grip things that are never meant for your attachment. Doing this keeps you as the one making everything happen and keeping everyone happy. You are not their source of happiness, and they are not yours. Feel the fulfillment of that and free yourself.

Ignore the outcome and results. You are here to thrive in bliss, love and abundance. Don't allow conditions to control you. You have a built-in spiritual guidance that is constantly directing your path. Yield to it. It stores your inspiring desires, dreams, future vision and infinite wisdom. Focus on the source of your inner reality and how good it feels now. Ignore your conditional reality of things that don't align with your vibrational inner reality. Tap into the Almighty all-knowing God in you.

"Do you not know that you are God's temple and that God's spirit dwells in you?" (1 Corinthians 3:16).

No matter what you're dealing with right now in your life you can connect to the infinite intelligence of the spirit of God that dwells in you and receive the guidance and direction you desire. Don't allow the details of your current life to mess up where you're going. It's a feeling of being happy and appreciative regardless of your condition. This is when you get to a level of focused joy and happiness knowing that everything is working for your good and living in this knowing.

There were times when I had to completely ignore certain things in my life that were demanding my attention. I had to completely distract myself with other things in order to manifest what I truly desired.

Relax, allow, enjoy and just be

Whatever that situation is that's been stressing you out, make the decision that you will completely distract yourself from the situation. As you ignore the unwanted condition give lots of attention and energy to the wanted attention and have fun in the process. For example, you may desire more money in your bank account but currently, your bank account balance reflects a number that is below your desires. However, you also have a vision of driving your dream car; distract yourself by going to a car dealer and test-driving your dream car. Visit different dealers and get in the car you desire. Have fun exploring the different cars while imagining yourself owning them and soon enough, not only will you attract your dream car but the money in your bank account will increase too.

The reason I can share this scenario with certainty and confidence is because it's my true story.

Focus on what you enjoy. No longer give attention to what you don't want. If the situation doesn't align with what you envision for yourself, don't give it your attention. No longer give attention to negative thinking. Where your attention goes, energy flows. It's so easy to get hung up on negative thinking and why bad things happen. But let me tell you again; like attracts like. Negative thinking will only attract negative outcomes. Focus on what brings you joy.

It's already done

Understand the very thing you desire is already done. You don't have to strive for it, stress over it or chase after it. It's already done. Things are shifting on your behalf. Make this commitment to yourself to no longer worry about what others think of you, how they judge you or what they think about your decisions. Feel the feeling of your desired manifestation. Feel the abundance, freedom, joy, ease, peace and clarity of it already being done. Ask yourself, now that it's already done, now what? Tell yourself, "I always get exactly what I want. I have all that I need. I have more than enough money to do exactly what I want to do when I want to do it. Speak these words over your situation. Speak abundance and life-giving words over your condition. Think thoughts that confirm your desired manifestation and stay far away from naysayers.

There will be people who doubt you, not understand you and even envy you. Stay focused. Don't get distracted by the negative energy. This process will require you to constantly ignore all negativity. Remember whatever you focus your attention on, your energy will flow. Look at it this way, your energy is your power. It's what charges you up. However, your energy runs low when it's not directed correctly. Just like your cell phone battery need to be charged up with more energy to function efficiently, you must charge your energy and direct it to things that benefit you the most. If your debt and bills don't serve you above all, why do you keep giving it so much energy by giving it your attention? If that toxic relationship is stressing you out and draining your energy, why does it keep getting your attention?

Instead, focus your energy on planning your dream trip, booking a weekend get-a-way retreat, writing a book, getting fit and having a healthier body. Focus your energy only on things that serve you and add to your life. As you direct your energy on what you enjoy, life becomes fun. You will feel differently. Life will feel more exciting and adventurous.

This is the key to your joy. It's prioritizing what feels good to you and making your happiness your main focus.

You may be thinking, but what about others? If I'm so focused on my own happiness, how can I support my family and others in need—isn't it selfish to prioritize my happiness?

No, it's not selfish. When you're happy, you have more to give to others. When you're thriving with joyful energy and deliberately keeping your attention on positive things that serve you, you are more fulfilled and equipped to have healthier relationships with others.

This is how you eliminate codependent relationships and self-sabotage, by knowing you are enough, and you are worthy of the best things life has to offer.

Appreciation

You may be thinking, "This seems difficult to do, I'm so used to putting others above myself." Appreciate where you are and allow yourself to gradually enhance your self-care habits. Being in a state of appreciation will take you far. You may not be where you want to be, but you can appreciate that even in the place of unwanted conditions you can still do something wanted. You may not be in your dream loving relationship, but you can appreciate the opportunity to envision experiences you desire to have with your soon-to-be love and feel the feelings that the love will bring. You can appreciate that you know what you desire in a partner and you're closer to attracting that love than ever before because you know strongly more than ever before exactly what you desire.

It's coming to the point of realizing that you don't get what you want, you get what you allow yourself to receive. What you desire doesn't take time; it takes alignment. Did you know there's a huge chance you are subconsciously blocking many of the blessings you desire in your life by not appreciating the manifested things all around you but instead focusing on the unwanted? It's when you stop yourself from receiving the good you really desire due to fear, unworthiness and low self-image. Attracting what you desire is so easy once you align yourself with all the joy, love and abundance life has to offer.

Make appreciation a priority in your life. You don't have to force anything. Just appreciate. Trust the process and allow your journey to unfold. Everything is working together for your good. Now surrender, allow and flow in your purpose. True happiness comes when you stop waiting for it and instead make the most of the moment you're in now to receive it. Take a deep breath and make the decision to appreciate your life.

You may not enjoy the few pounds you gained and really desire to get fit. Appreciate the fact that you can gradually add more exercise and healthier foods into your daily routine. Just start moving toward the desired outcome while ignoring the current unwanted conditions.

The very thing you desire is on its way. It may not come in the way you expect it, and it may not come in the time you thought it would but it's unfolding now. Things are shifting for you; people are moving out the way.

God is orchestrating the details on your behalf. Trust the process. To your natural mind, it doesn't make sense. But it's perfectly understood by your inner being.

Go within, get quiet, get clear and allow yourself to be guided from within. Don't be distracted by unfavorable conditions. They are fading out. Abide in the shadow of the almighty. You are divine.

JOURNAL

——————— ❧❦❧ ———————

Feel the feeling of your desired manifestation. Feel the abundance, freedom, joy, ease, peace and clarity of it already being done. Ask yourself, now that it's already done, now what?

_____

_____

_____

_____

_____

What do you desire to manifest? How will you begin to focus your energy?

_____

_____

_____

_____

_____

"Put your energy only on things that serve you and add to your life. As you direct your energy on what you enjoy, life becomes fun."

CHAPTER 6

EVOLVING TO THE STATE OF KNOWING

People will always have an opinion about you. People have various preferences about who they accept and what they like. Even your parents and close family members. They have an idea of who they believe you to be. They will place you in categories in their mind in order to comprehend and understand you. However, as you evolve into who you desire to be it may not fit in with what they believe you to be. As you do the inner work of healing (mind, body and spirit) and evolve as a happier healthy person, there may be times when people project their own trauma onto you just to bring you down to a level they're more comfortable with. This is why it's important to be happy without another person's validation. This is a level of power and freedom no one can ever take from you— it's when you stop caring what people think about you. When you stop caring about results and outcomes and you become focused to live a joyous life without the need for external validation. People often struggle and have a hard time accepting the new. As you focus and evolve into the new you, there will be major shifts in your life that reflect this new you. You will begin to enjoy your life more and embrace all the wonderful transformations. However, this evolvement may cause some people to feel uncomfortable around the change. They may feel like you left them. Your joy, happiness and success may cause them to compare their struggles to your satisfaction. Don't allow this to discourage you or cause guilt due to your success. Remember you succeeding does not take away from them.

"You can't become poor enough to help the poor, just as you can't become sick enough to help the sick." – Esther Hicks

Embrace your happiness, prosperity, joy and abundance. Appreciate all of it and enjoy every moment. You are in this world to enjoy life abundantly and when you give yourself permission to do so, it liberates others to do the same.

Think of a tree. A tree is unmovable. It stands tall and firm bearing fruit. A tree doesn't care whether or not you enjoy the fruit it bears. The tree is doing what it's destined to do. That's the way you must be. Focus on doing what you're destined to do, just be. Stop caring about what other people think about you and focus on falling in love with the best version of yourself. Become your own best friend. When you criticize yourself and doubt your capabilities you become your own enemy and that thinking leads you to be at war with yourself. Don't be the weapon formed against yourself that is causing you not to prosper. Instead, encourage yourself, cheer yourself on and become your biggest supporter by investing in yourself. Let go of your past and stop allowing what happened to you to hold you hostage of prospering in the present moment. Let go of the opinions, thoughts and criticism of others and stay true to what's best for your evolvement and life expansion. Begin to fall in love with doing your own thing. Minding your own business and manifesting in your own lane. You don't have to do it the way they did it. You don't have to appeal to what other people like. You don't have to live to please them. You don't have to travel in their lane, beat to their drum and ride their bandwagon. Embrace the authenticity of you.

Imagination

Your imagination is your connection to God.

"So God created mankind in his own image, in the image of God he created him; male and female he created them" (Genesis 1:27).

God imagined you first and now you are physically manifested. When you use your imagination, you are doing the very thing that God did in creating you. Imagination is the first step to manifesting. What do you imagine for your life? Do you have images of prospering in your future? Anytime you image positive, loving and wonderful things you are aligned to the desires God has for your life. Allow yourself to imagine. The following are the steps to manifesting.

Manifesting Formula:

- Imagine what you want
- Ask, write it down
- Allow the feeling of it
- Connect to intuition and take inspired action
- Evolve from believing to knowing
- Receive.

If you're interested in getting more guidance beyond this book, I invite you to join my 21-Day Manifesting Bootcamp. This Bootcamp includes exclusive videos with me guiding you through the process, daily journaling, meditation and affirmation audios and life scripting tools. Sign up at www.ManifestWithRainie.com.

SIS, BE NICER TO YOURSELF

After you have imagined what you want, and you ask in prayer and write it down the manifestation process begins. It's important to write the vision/imagination. Writing it down puts the imagined desire on physical paper and into the atmosphere of the universe. This allows you to let go of trying to overthink it and trying to figure it out. This process doesn't need so much mental attention. As a matter of fact, the mental attention will often push the desire away.

Stop believing and start knowing

So, write it down and release it. After that's complete focus on how you are feeling—not about the feelings of the desire but allowing yourself to feel good. When you feel good you attract good. Positive feelings become a positive vibrational force that will attract positive experiences back into your life. Do things that align with your natural state of peace and calm. Life doesn't need to be a struggle. If you do things that bring joy, your dreams will manifest more quickly. As you care more about how you feel and keeping your vibes high, you will become more aware of your intuition. Your intuition is your inner guidance to your unique path of manifesting. You will begin to receive gut feelings that inspire you to take action. As you continue to fine-tune this process you will witness yourself evolving from believing in your desired manifestation to knowing it's already done before you physically see it. This leveling of knowing is the highest level of faith. It's a firm certainty that is unwavering and no matter what conditions look like nothing can interfere with the deep knowing that it's done. This leveling of manifesting positions you to easily and effortlessly receive.

Be consistent

Repetition creates habits and habits shape destiny. When you do something over and over again it becomes you and you master it. As you apply the manifestation formula to your life create consistency. Repetition builds mastery to your manifestations.

When I first learned about the process of manifestation, I started building repetition with daily habits. These habits reinforced good feelings and high vibe energy which resulted in attracting better experiences, thoughts and relationships in my life. I consistently followed a morning routine to nurture my mind, body and spirit. I am still committed to this routine although it has evolved. I start my day off with a meditation, visualization and sometimes gratitude journaling. Then after getting ready and eating breakfast, I exercise my body and listen to audiobooks, podcasts or motivational messages to empower my mind.

This morning routine sets my entire day. I've learned years ago if you master your morning, you will master your day, if you master your day, you will master your week. As you master your week you will master your year and as you master your years you will master your entire life. Small daily habits create big life-evolving experiences. However, it requires your consistent commitment regardless of the conditional outcome. When it comes to allowing and trusting the process, discipline yourself to not be moved, bothered and upset when things don't go as expected. When it seems that people do you wrong or are unfair don't allow it to impact your good feelings. Instead, trust that it's all working together for a greater purpose. Don't let situations cause you to feel like a victim or even feel mistreated. Don't allow yourself to believe in unfair treatment; instead, believe that everything is always working together in your favor even when it doesn't logically make sense. Hold on to that belief, it will all be worth it when the manifestation unfolds. Become more focused on the feeling, vibes and energy you desire and less on the specific conditions bringing the feeling. That's how you stay aligned to the manifestation no matter what the condition is.

Stay committed to holding on to your high vibe and positive energy even when it comes to being around others who don't reflect positive energy. As you remain consistent it will get easier and easier to feel good all the time and direct your life regardless of external conditions.

You lack nothing

You will soon get to a place where you will not need to convince or prove anything to anyone. You will determine you don't need another person to do a particular thing before something manifests in your life. It shall manifest with or without the participation of a specific person. Make the decision to radiate love and joy and allow yourself to just be. You don't need the approval of others. You lack nothing so eliminate the desperate energy of being needy. Learn to keep your silence and become quieter about what you're believing for. Your vision isn't for everyone to hear. When you operate this way, you flow in powerful energy. You begin to understand that there are no real problems, issues or challenges when you do get energy and attention to them. Many people are going throughout life expanding their problems because they talk about them to others and constantly analyze them. If you don't want it, don't give it your attention. Problems don't really exist. It's just life and the things that are happening are often setting you up to be ready for what you really desire. The more you allow and prioritize feeling good, the more you will be opened to gracefully receive your heart desires.

"And let endurance have its perfect result and do a thorough work, so that you may be perfect and completely developed in your faith, lacking in nothing" (James 1:4).

You lack nothing. Even when it comes to love, you have no lack. Don't allow loneliness to reconnect you to toxic relationships. It's just like drinking poison because you're thirsty. Every time you go back to that toxic relationship you set yourself back and you keep retaking the same test and experiencing the same disappointment of the failure results. However, keeping your standards high, (because you lack nothing) protects you from settling for less and eliminates low-quality experiences. Why settle for less than what you really desire? Even if most of the people around you are settling, and even if it's common to settle, that does not mean settling for less is what you should do. It takes courage to have standards and stick to them. Some people will try to convince you to settle because that's all they know. It doesn't mean that they are jealous or that they want you to suffer, sometimes it's because that's all they know to do. This is why you have to focus on what's best for you and only you can know what's best for you and what standards to set in your life. When you discover them maintain those standards even when others try to talk you out of them. Because at the end of the day, this is your life—live it fully.

JOURNAL

———— ✎✐✎✐ ————

What is the vision you desire to manifest in your life? Write it down.

_____

_____

_____

_____

_____

What are the daily habits you plan to repetitiously implement? How will you consistently maintain your faith and certainty throughout the manifestation process?

_____

_____

_____

_____

_____

"When you feel good you attract good. Positive feelings become a positive vibrational force that will attract positive experiences back into your life."

CHAPTER 7

MAINTAINING YOUR DESIRED MANIFESTATION

Once you experience physical manifestation of your desire you will go through three phases. The first phase is excitement and shock; you may feel like you can't believe it's finally here and part of your reality. During this phase, you will feel very excited and grateful. The second phase is analyzing and reviewing the details. During this phase, some people feel disappointed and may think, "All this time I put so much energy and attention to this manifestation and this is it?" You didn't know what to expect but you realize quickly that the excitement of the physical manifestation is very brief compared to the level of alignment required to attract it.

This is the reason some wealthy people and famous celebrities say that material possessions don't create happiness. The issue is having put all your attention and energy toward something that empowered you and kept you focused and once you receive it, there's nothing left to focus on, and you feel a lack of purpose because of it. You are striving for that thing that gave you a sense of focus and purpose but once it's received, your ego is tempted to feel as if you've arrived, however, life continues to go on. So, you ask yourself, "What's next?" But part of you does not know how to relax and enjoy what is because you've become addicted to the chase of what's next. The healthy way of maintaining success is a combination of appreciating what is while allowing the guidance of what's next. What's next will flow naturally. Just as you naturally evolved as a baby, toddler, young child and now an adult, your next level manifestation is flowing naturally as ideas, individual relationship connections, material possessions and opportunities.

The last phase you experience after your physical manifestation is acceptance. Maintain a state of accepting what is and what is to come. Accept it as you desire it to be. Some people never settle into this final phase of acceptance and instead, their old mindset and thought patterns of doubt and fear cloud their vision. Instead of accepting their new norm of their desired manifestation, they fear losing it and doubt the evolvement of anything better. Keeping yourself in a state of appreciation, ease, gratitude and abundance is important. When you manifest something new in your life, it's helpful to give yourself time to settle into the feeling of it and savor its presence. Rushing forward to what's next and forcing the outcome of what will cause energies of stress and anxiety to expand in your life. Celebrate your small and large wins, take a significant amount of time off the rest and rejuvenate after large manifestations. Give your mind the space to comprehend everything and allow yourself to spiritually and emotionally process everything. Be intentional about giving thanks to God and honoring everyone and everything that aligned to support the manifestation. Allow yourself the grace and space to become one with your new norm. This process of taking ownership of your new level of norm should not be rushed, just like the manifestation process was not rushed.

Imposter Syndrome

Skipping the process of taking ownership of your manifestation can often lead to a battle in your mind. You may feel like you're not good enough and people will expose you any moment. It may seem like other people are doing great with their success and they have everything figured out, but you are faking it. You may even struggle with thoughts of not being capable. These negative thoughts lead to patterns of negative self-talk and self-image. This experience is often called imposter syndrome.

Understand, you are not your thoughts. Just because you think something doesn't mean it's true. It's time to get out of your own way and take ownership of your success.

"Sometimes we become captive to our thoughts and past thinking." – Patrick Howard

Carrying past thinking is just like carrying heavy baggage you need to get rid of. You overcome this toxic thinking by becoming intentional about thinking positively. Here are a few things you can begin doing to overcome negative thoughts:

- Make a daily practice of speaking positive affirmations
- Practice meditating daily
- Enjoy music and dancing
- Get out in nature.

Learn to focus on what you enjoy instead of what you dislike. No longer give attention to negativity. Focus your attention on the good. It's easy to get hung up on negative thinking and why bad things happen. But let me tell you again; like attracts like. Negative thinking will only attract negative outcomes. Create a habit of celebrating your small wins and counting your blessings and stop comparing yourself to others. Understand you can deliberately decide to enjoy your life, be happy and appreciate your own moment. You have the power to do this one moment at a time. You can speak life over your situation and know that you are worthy and deserving of good things. Make that decision each day to be positive, to love unconditionally and to focus on the good. Embrace the life you desire and not the negative manifestations of temporary conditions. See them as fleeting and maintain your commitment to embracing your new norm of joy, love, abundance and happiness. Allow yourself to settle into the fullest of life you desire. True abundance is a state of mind, it is intentional purpose with little to no hard work. It's effortless, it comes with ease. It doesn't require a struggle for your divine vision to unfold and manifest into miracles and blessings that remind you that everything really is working in your favor. Joy and bliss are where manifestations happen; not in worry, stress and struggle. It happens living a joyful life.

"Faith and fear both demand you believe in something you cannot see. You choose!" – Bob Proctor

If you will let go of the energy of control that forces and fights conditions and instead align yourself to allow the flow of God—the divine source of infinite intelligence—to guide you then you can easily and effortlessly experience life abundantly. Happiness comes when you stop waiting for it and instead make the most of the moment you're in now to receive it. Whatever you pay attention to, you buy that experience. If you allow yourself to focus on something that upsets you, you feed it your energy and it reciprocates more experiences of you being upset. Always live from the energy as if what you desire has already materialized in the physical realm. Feel as if it's already done.

JOURNAL

——————— ❧☙❧☙ ———————

How you ever experienced imposter syndrome by having a feeling of not being good enough or feeling like you're fake and not capable of good?

_____

_____

_____

_____

_____

What will you start doing to overcome negative thoughts?

_____

_____

_____

_____

_____

"Happiness comes when you stop waiting for it and instead make the most of the moment you're in now to receive it."

CONCLUSION

God is evolving you, moving you to greater, higher levels of experiences. As you stay connected to your vision and purpose you will not be moved by unfavorable external things and conditions. Don't look to external things for divine guidance. Look within, infinite intelligence dwells in you. Evolving to this new level in your life will require you to trust the process. Sometimes the growth process will cause you to end relationships, remove some habits and even walk away from plans. Regardless of where this evolvement brings you, remember you never need to convince or prove anything to anyone. You don't need another person to do a particular thing and you don't need a specific thing to happen. Stop waiting for life to give you the permission to be happy and give yourself permission by deciding to be happy now. What God has for you is for you and no one can stop it. It's already done, receive it.

If you're interested in getting more guidance beyond this book, I invite you to join my 21-Day Manifesting Bootcamp. This Bootcamp includes exclusive videos with me guiding you through the process, daily journaling, meditation and affirmation audios and life scripting tools. Sign up at www.ManifestWithRainie.com

ARE YOU ADDICTED TO A TOXIC LOVE?

The obsession of a toxic relationship can have the same enticement as drugs or alcohol. The pattern echoes time and time again: a new significant other draws you into a new relationship that starts off lovingly and alluringly only to develop into a hurtful or abusive cycle. A person with a healthy understanding of "true love" does not tolerate this kind of pain. He or she will move on in search of a healthier bond. It's an unhealthy view of love that will rationalize in toxic behavior and make another person cling to a relationship long after it should have ended. Like any other addiction, those hooked on toxic love have little or no control over excessive urges to text, call, manipulate or beg for love, attention and affection. They want help. They want to end the pain and recover, but it's much like trying to shake a drug habit. Get your copy at http://bit.ly/AddictedToPain

Have you been trapped in a constant cycle of toxic relationships that have you frustrated with your love life?

Do you feel fear, insecurity and anxiety that have you

asking yourself "Am I enough?"

You Are Enough takes readers on an incredible journey of self-understanding to explore the root causes of negative emotions projecting themselves in their outside relationships.

The concept that the fear of never finding true love and consistently trying to please others are major factors for the engagement in toxic relationships. By addressing the fear and anxiety you feel inside, Rainie helps you discover your true self-worth, which is sure to change your life!

Get your copy at http://bit.ly/YouAreEnoughBook

HAVE YOU BEEN PRAYING FOR A HUSBAND?

It's not easy being single, and when you have a vision to be

 married, it's challenging to patiently wait for the right one. It's important to understand that God has a divine purpose for your life, and He wants to gift you with the right man. *When God Sent My Husband* is a single

women's guide to gaining wisdom on:

- How to guard your heart yet freely love
- Preparing and positioning yourself to receive love
- Building a solid foundation that captures and sustains love

In this book, Rainie Howard shares her personal story of searching for love, dating and embracing the divine experience of God bringing her husband into her life. This is a miraculous story of God being the ultimate matchmaker. The book will encourage you to take a spiritual approach towards dating and preparing for marriage. Get your copy at http://bit.ly/WhenGodSentMyHusband

EVER FELT STUCK OR WEIGHED DOWN BY THE PRESSURES OF LIFE?

No matter how hard you try, you just can't get unstuck.

It's like sitting in a car, pushing down on the accelerator as hard as you can, and the car never starts moving. You are running in the race of life, but you're getting nowhere. Doors are constantly closing, opportunities are nowhere to be found, and you can't get your breakthrough. You've tried everything, but nothing seems to work. You are in desperate need of an "Undeniable Breakthrough!" Whether you need a breakthrough in your relationship, career, finances or health, this spiritual guide will give you all the life strategies needed to experience the blessings of an undeniable breakthrough. Get your copy at http://bit.ly/UndeniableBreakthrough

Did you know that anxiety, depression, and fear stem from emotional experiences you keep tucked away in your heart?

Often, people who struggle with anxiety, depression, worry, and fear are left with a sense of hopelessness. They become entangled in a battle against their own emotions,

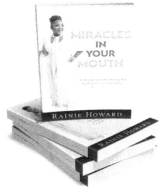

giving way to confusion, stress, and even panic attacks. As isolation sets in, its whispering doubts make people believe they are alone, misunderstood, and sometimes even unloved. The good news is you can find hope and healing in life's darkest moments. In *Miracles in Your Mouth*, you will learn the spiritual strategy to heal, renew, and transform your life. God wants to unleash His power, protection, and prosperity upon you. Will you accept it? Bestselling author Rainie Howard shares the mysteries of covenant prayer, powerful affirmations, and divine declarations to strengthen your mind, heal your emotions, and renew your spirit.

Get your copy at www.MiraclesInYourMouth.com

WHAT DO YOU DO WHEN THE LOVE FADES?

It's supposed to be love but in those rare moments it feels

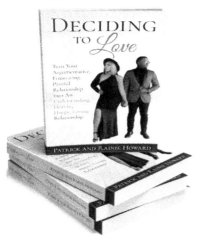

like pain. You're supposed to be happy, and, on the outside, everything looks good, but the truth is deep down inside you are wondering if it will last.

What do you do when the love fades, when the commitment wavers and when you're not sure if you will stay in a relationship? How do you endure the challenges of the heart and the feelings of frustration that makes you want to quit? How do you get through the hurtful emotions, the resentment and the fears that hold you hostage? How do you stop replaying the disappointing past that seems to define your present moment? You're confused and uncertain about what's next. You don't know why things blow up so badly and the rage, pain and anger get out of control. Where does it come from? Where has it been hiding all that time and when will it come back? Will next time be worst?